DATE DUE		

MAR 10

CARING

by Jane Belk Moncure
illustrated by Helen Endres

THE CHILD'S WORLD

MANKATO, MN 56001

Library of Congress Cataloging in Publication Data

Moncure, Jane Belk.
  Caring.

  (What is it?)
  SUMMARY: Presents ways a child can show caring
behavior.
  1. Caring—Juvenile literature. (1. Caring)
I. Endres, Helen. II. Title
BF575.L8M565 1981   177'.7   80-27506
ISBN 0-89565-201-3 -1991 Edition

CARING

What is caring?

When I hold my little brother on my shoulders so he can pick apples too, that's caring.

When I help a turtle across a path
in the park so he will be safe, that's
caring.

Caring is feeding the wild birds—
not just when it snows, but all winter
long!

Caring is picking up paper and trash
someone else left under the picnic table.
Caring is putting them where they belong.

When a friend asks for another push in the swing; and it's the tenth push and you do it anyway, that's caring.

When you leave wild flowers to
bloom along a mountain trail so others
can enjoy them too, that's caring.

When you put your bicycle in the garage so it won't get wet or stolen, that's caring.

Caring is teaching a friend how to turn
a cartwheel.

Caring is wrapping your coat around a
friend on a chilly day.

When you make up your bed,

put your clothes away,

and keep your toys picked up, without
being asked again and again, that's
caring.

Caring is helping Dad plant a new tree
after a storm knocked down the old one.

When you get a bandage for a friend
who scraped her knee, that's caring.

When you feed and brush your puppy
and give him clean water every day,
that's caring.

When you faithfully pick up your
bowl and glass and spoon, and carry
them to the sink, that's caring.

Caring is being a friend to a new
person in the neighborhood.

Believe it or not, caring is listening to your parents and trying to do the things they ask you to do.

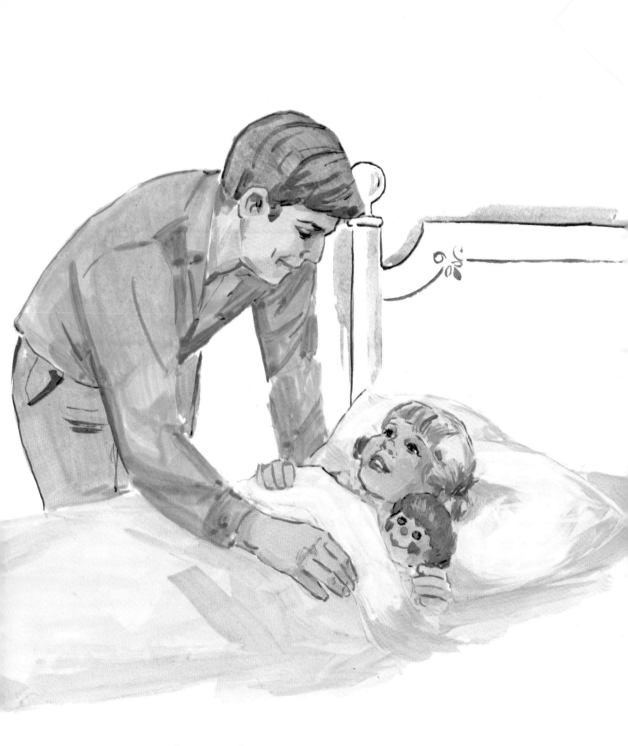

They ask because they care.

Can you think of other ways to show caring?

About the Author:

Jane Belk Moncure, author of many books and stories for young children, is a graduate of Virginia Commonwealth University and Columbia University. She has taught nursery, kindergarten and primary children in Europe and America. Mrs. Moncure has taught early childhood education while serving on the faculties of Virginia Commonwealth University and the University of Richmond. She was the first president of the Virginia Association for Early Childhood Education and has been recognized widely for her services to young children. She is married to Dr. James A. Moncure, Vice President of Elon College, and currently lives in Burlington, North Carolina.

About the Artist:

Helen Endres is a commercial artist, designer and illustrator of children's books. She has lived and worked in the Chicago area since coming from her native Oklahoma in 1952. Graduated from Tulsa University with a BA, she received further training at Hallmark in Kansas City and from the Chicago Art Institute. Ms. Endres attributes much of her creative achievement to the advice and encouragement of her Chicago contemporaries and to the good humor and patience of the hundreds of young models who have posed for her.